Migrants and Militants

T0087470

Migrants and Militants

Alain Badiou

Translated by Joseph Litvak

polity

Polity Press
65 Bridge Street
Cambridge CB2 1UR, UK

Polity Press
101 Station Landing
Suite 300
Medford, MA 02155, USA

ISBN-13: 978-1-5095-4245-1
ISBN-13: 978-1-5095-4246-8 - paperback

A catalogue record for this book is available from the British Library.

Library of Congress Cataloging-in-Publication Data
Names: Badiou, Alain, author. | Litvak, Joseph, translator.
Title: Migrants and militants / Alain Badiou ; translated by Joseph Litvak.
Other titles: Méfiez-vous des Blancs, habitants du rivage. English
Description: Cambridge ; Medford, MA : Polity, [2020] | "Originally
    published in French as Méfiez-vous des blancs, habitants du rivage!
    ©Librairie Arthème Fayard, 2019." | Includes bibliographical
    references. | Summary: "France's leading philosopher gives a powerful
    account of our obligations to migrants"-- Provided by publisher.
Identifiers: LCCN 2019047001 (print) | LCCN 2019047002 (ebook) | ISBN
    9781509542451 (hardback) | ISBN 9781509542468 (paperback) | ISBN
    9781509542475 (epub)
Subjects: LCSH: Emigration and immigration. | Refugees. | Other
    (Philosophy)
Classification: LCC JV6035 .B3413 2020 (print) | LCC JV6035 (ebook) | DDC
    305.9/0691--dc23
LC record available at https://lccn.loc.gov/2019047001
LC ebook record available at https://lccn.loc.gov/2019047002

Typeset in 12.5 on 15 pt Adobe Garamond by Servis Filmsetting Ltd, Stockport, Cheshire
Printed and bound in Great Britain by CPI Group (UK) Ltd, Croydon

For further information on Polity, visit our website:
politybooks.com

The first version of this text was a lecture given at the Maison de la Poésie in Paris. The idea for this evening came from the Textes & Voix group, directed by Nadine Eghels.

I place at the threshold of this book a 'Madagascan Song', written in 1783 by Évaryste de Parny, apparently inspired by Madagascan traditions. The song shows – and this is good news – that a radical, indeed violent anti-colonialism is as old as colonialism itself. Maurice Ravel, who was himself a true progressive, and who in particular supported the Bolsheviks, took this text, in 1926, as the basis for a superb melody.

A.B.

Beware of the white men,
You dwellers on the shore.
In the time of our fathers,
White men descended on this island.
One said to them: here is land,
May your wives cultivate it;
Be just, be good,
And become our brothers.

The white men promised, and yet
They built entrenchments.
A menacing fort arose;
The thunder was enclosed
In brass canons;
Their priests wanted to give us
A God that we did not know;
They spoke at last
Of obedience and of slavery.
Sooner death!
The carnage was long and terrible;
But despite the lightning that they vomited,
And that crushed whole armies,
They were all exterminated.
Beware of the white men!

We saw new tyrants,
Stronger and more numerous,
Plant their flag on the shore:
The sky fought for us;
It made rain fall on them,
Tempests and poisonous winds.
They are no more, and we live free.
Beware of the white men,
You dwellers on the shore.

'Madagascan Song', Évaryste de Parny

In certain situations, apparently, one issue can have the power to wipe away another, which had until then seemed to be the most important one.

We all know that the so-called question of immigration, of migrants, of foreigners, of refugees, was until very recently a question that divided – and could divide even very seriously, and in all sorts of practical ways – public opinion in France, in Europe, and finally in the entire so-called western world – that is, in all the privileged countries on our planet. It could be argued that, for a mere handful of weeks now, in France the question of the yellow vests [*gilets jaunes*] has swept aside the so-called 'migrant' question in the terrors as well as in the enthusiasms of public opinion.

In fact there is a sense in which the question of the yellow vests is exactly the opposite of the so-called migrant question. What is at stake here, essentially, is the destiny of an old France that finds itself threatened. First of all, there are the low-level civil servants, the artisans, the shopkeepers, the small businesspeople, and the farmers, who are revolting against the obvious decline in their status and income and are anxious and angry, given the general lack of interest in their condition and the contempt in which they are held by the transnational oligarchy that runs global capitalism today. This is about stricken lands and territories, about provincial cities that have been turned into ghost towns, about the world of hunting and town meetings. But there is also a vast suburban lower-middle class, and in particular the large number of retired people it contains who, as they struggle to make ends meet, glimpse the spectre of their pauperization, of their proletarianization. This is ultimately about a world in which one can see and feel a very real abandonment by the state powers, themselves subordinate to the powers of capital – an abandonment in which one can also decipher the slow and geo-logical decay into which both Europe and the so-called western democratic world are slipping today. What is being abandoned is the old, mori-bund, provincial world, at once suburban and colonial, that the bright young graduates at the top business and administrative schools couldn't care less about – and Macron is their prototype.

We thus have a confrontation between global modernity in the form of an arrogant and ulti-mately criminal oligarchy on the one side and, on the other, the archaism of an understandable nationwide reaction, driven by that part of soci-ety whose little privileges, long in place, are being threatened by the deployment of contemporary capitalism. France, a waning little imperial power up against monsters such as the United States and China, is no longer capable of buying, at a reasonable price in wages, public services, and 'social advantages', the support of the lower middle classes, which have always been the cen-tral resource of our famous 'democracies'.

Inevitably, then, we have on one side the state, obedient to the needs of the global market and its handful of billionaires, and on the other side a movement of protest that seems to represent the working class but whose political vision is vague, timid (it carefully avoids the heart of the problem, namely private ownership of the means of production and international competition), nationalistic (at a moment when France represents an investment without a future) fabricated out of false rumours, and whose only truly organized parliamentary component is the far right.

In itself, this sort of conflict offers strictly nothing that could ever lead – that could ever lead us – beyond the sheer persistence of the same dominant structures tediously repeating themselves. This is the price we pay for the near absence, from the asymmetrical conflict that preoccupies us today, of the only other possible way, the way that has the potential to be at once modern and egalitarian: the communist way, to call it by its name. For I have never been able to find any other, despite exhortations from all sides not to use a word that the mass media have rendered unspeakable.

That said, whatever attention we give to this narrowly national situation or to the risks we can discern in a conflict that opposes two protagonists, neither of whom has any political coherence or offers any promise of an egalitarian future, we must at least insist on the inherent internationalism of any new and affirmative political vision. We must insist that the scene of old France belongs to the past, and we must hold on to the conviction that anything truly important today comes down to this: that the point of departure for our thinking must be the world, the whole world. For Marx's aphorism according to which 'proletarians have no homeland' is even truer today – truer for us today, necessarily, than it was in Marx's time. In other words, our homeland is the world, and our compatriots make up working humankind in all its diversity.

This takes us back to the so-called migrants, who represent the arrival and the presence, among our people, of this infinite diversity and of everything that comes from elsewhere. They are the sign that, because our homeland is becoming theirs without their origin being denied, we must also – 'we' standing for the communist politics of our time – expatriate ourselves in the direction of the expatriated; we must, like them, have no other political homeland than the one demanded by our common work.

I want to let them speak now about the word

'migrant'. This is a declaration made by a young person, still a minor, who arrived here in France with many others, not long ago, and whose country of origin is Guinea. We will not say anything more about him, as precautions require. Here is what he had to say about the word with which we are concerned:

To me, 'migrant' seems like a word that was created just to hurt the people who understand its true meaning. Otherwise, why not use existing words, by saying 'foreigners'? Because, in our country, if you're French, we're not going to say you're a 'migrant'. Anyway, you're no longer in your country. You're in a foreign country. But we say, 'he's French'. Just to differentiate him from the Guineans. We say, 'that person is European; that one is French; that one is English; that one is Spanish'. We refer to him or her by his or her country. We don't say that he's 'expatriated'. We don't say that she's a 'migrant'. We don't say that he's a 'refugee'. Even if you're a political refugee, because years ago there were wars in the sub-region of West Africa. Everyone from those countries came and took refuge in Guinea, but we didn't call them 'refugees'. These are words that are used by some people, but not by most people. That is, we just say, 'they're from Sierra Leone', or 'they're Liberians'. We don't need to say that they're 'refugees' or 'migrants'. These days, I'm thinking that the word 'migrant' is just for us Africans, because the word 'migrant' started when people started coming to Europe from Africa, via the Mediterranean.

I don't think of myself so much as a 'migrant'. Anyone who says 'migrant' doesn't really understand the meaning of the word. I mean, I think 'migrant' is for animals. It's animals that migrate. You can see that. People say: 'The migration of animals has led to this or that.' I think the word 'migrant' shouldn't be used for people who fled their country so as not to be mistreated. There are also people who may have fled their country because things weren't going well, the economic problem. We can call them 'refugees'. But even the word 'refugee' doesn't seem to me to have any room for a human being.

I'd like to tell people who think of themselves as 'migrants' that all they have to do is think of themselves as foreigners. I can agree to that word, because we're not talking about your homeland. Yes, you're a foreigner. When you're a foreigner, you're a foreigner. But, whatever your nature, you should never let them call you a 'migrant'. The word 'migrant' is just to get people all worked up. It's just to stir up contempt. That's all. No one has ever called a white

7

man a 'migrant'. Ever! So, really, the word 'migrant' shouldn't exist today. 'Migrant' is just for blacks who leave Africa to go to Europe.[1]

Reading this strong statement, we might think that the case is closed, that the word 'migrant' has been condemned. But the history of this whole matter is much more complicated.

Let us recall a few facts that are often forgotten about the history of the arrival and settlement in France of several million foreigners, now spread out across our cities, often going back three generations. We can clearly distinguish several moments:

- From the 1950s to the 1970s, French industry, rebuilding itself and growing rapidly, has to import at all costs a labour force greater than that provided by the exodus from the country to the city. Companies fly all over the Maghreb, then all over sub-Saharan Africa, looking for workers. More than a million Portuguese come to work in France. No one speaks of immigration as a problem; instead, people speak of workers. A great many 'workers' hostels' are built to house this labour force.

All this is kept going by the fact that French capitalism is for the most part a state capitalism. Well-known factories such as Renault Billancourt are state properties. Whole sectors, from energy to transport to communications, are nationalized. The Bank of France enjoys no independence from the state, and many banks are nationalized. As a result of all this, we can speak of an 'international proletariat of France' – as we did in the organization to which I belonged at the end of the 1960s.

- From the late 1970s and the early 1980s on, we start to see, as an effect of the pressures of the global market on a diminished imperial France, the dismantling of the state monopoly capitalism that characterized our country. This movement of privatization in fact goes along with massive deindustrialization. With the disappearance of the great factories, the areas around the big cities change completely, in both appearance and population. People now start talking not about workers any more, but about immigrants. And an uncertain period begins for the fate of the working-class populations of the older suburbs. The dominant and official idea about so-called immigrants is that they are not, indeed cannot be, inhabitants of this country like everyone else, with the same rights. The debate rages, while a few regularizations of status are arranged – but also while closed systems are put in place that announce real acts of segregation.

• From the 1990s until today, a veritable ideological counter-revolution has made immigrants and immigration a supposedly major political 'problem'. It is here that the word 'migrant' appears, after 'worker' and 'immigrant'. The nationalistic and fascistic theme of the foreigner as a quasi-racial threat becomes almost as active as it was in the 1930s. The supporters of this counter-revolution do not hesitate to portray the situation as that of an invasion of our civilized countries by hordes (the example being the 'Roma') – hordes of 'migrants', that is. The Muslim religion is considered to be a barbaric peril. Workers' hostels are closed; young people in working-class suburbs are placed under police surveillance; deportation becomes the norm; obtaining a residence permit becomes a nightmare; thousands of so-called migrants are left to drown in the Mediterranean; hateful new laws are passed that end up targeting the people concerned even at the level of the clothes they wear and the food they eat.

So we arrive at the situation we are in today, where the positions taken on the question of people of foreign origin, of people who were, or would like to continue to be, part of the international proletariat of France, of people whom we see on construction sites, or collecting garbage, or working in restaurants, in the cleaning business, in public transport, in plumbing, in hotel-keeping, in the great annual harvests of wine and fruit, in services to the elderly, in taking care of children or cleaning apartments – yes, everything we think, say, and do about them has gradually marked out an ideological boundary, has gradually become an essential motive for division and conflict in our decadent society, which does not want to know how decadent it is or to draw firm and carefully thought through political conclusions from that knowledge.

All this is to say that there is a choice about the bad word 'migrant', and one that it is impossible to evade. There is a dividing line, a stage of ambivalence, a moment where I have to choose between inertia and action, and also between my stable identity and the provocation that the arrival of the other represents for it, his insistence on being here and on calling for my brotherhood.

The bad word 'migrant' leads us to reflections like these.

By writing the book entitled *Migrant Brothers*, the great writer Patrick Chamoiseau has in a sense transformed this bad word, charged it with poetry. He suggests from the beginning of this book that what is at stake in it is speaking about a cause that is in fact merciless, demanding that we act. Here are his words:

Here, close by (almost so far away), they are dispersed, they are punished with arrests, rocks are stacked and barriers raised in spaces dedicated to their final weariness; over there, far away (almost so close), coastguards, wall guards, border guards – *guards of life, guards of death!* – are sick of not being able to contain them! ... The flow has the vitality of a biblical beginning, it swells having never begun, it begins again having never slowed down and even before it had time to stop ... At times, guards of misery machine-gun madly and randomly, and often torture out of exasperation, and when they find themselves driven to the limits of their own conscience they cry without really understanding why! ...

She then growls with all her youth: *Islamophobia insecurity identity immigration ... are words that have turned monstrous!* They've mated under media hypnosis, in a shrill horde, and they grind madly like cogs, in almost every direction, everywhere, almost endlessly, crushing people under bright city lights and boulevard garlands! ... We have to act, here's a cause![2]

Yes, this much is clear: here's a cause, and we have to act.

I would like to examine the current state of this issue by looking at two positive but different orientations, and by doing so with the help of two equally different thought procedures: poetry and political analysis.

Let me suggest these two orientations right away. I will call the first orientation ethical, and its fundamental concept is the other, the human other. The essential norm of this orientation is hospitality. I will call the second orientation communist. Its fundamental concept is that of the proletariat, and its essential norm is transnational organization.

In order to lay out the stakes of these two orientations, I will use political and philosophical texts, but also poems.

As far as the ethical orientation is concerned, I think we can sum it up as follows: welcoming the foreigner is a duty that transcends all laws. Therefore one speaks here at the level of a personal relation between the one who arrives and the one who is already living here. Welcoming the one who comes is, then, an ethical obligation and, like any ethical obligation, is unconditional.

Here is how the philosopher Jacques Derrida presents the ethical orientation, whose maxim is, we must say 'yes' to the one who arrives, whoever that person may be:

> Let us say yes *to who or what turns up*, before any determination, before any anticipation, before any *identification*, whether or not it has to do with a foreigner, an immigrant, an invited guest, or an unexpected visitor, whether or not the new arrival is the citizen of another country, a human, an animal, or divine creature, a living or dead thing, male or female.

In other words, there would be an antinomy, an insoluble antinomy, a non-dialectizable antinomy between, on the one hand, *the* law of unlimited hospitality (to give the new arrival all of one's home and oneself, to give him or her one's own, our own, without asking a name, or compensation, or the fulfilment of even the smallest condition), and, on the other hand, the *laws* (in the plural), those rights and duties that are always conditioned, and conditioned as they are defined by the Greco-Roman tradition and even the Judeo-Christian one, by all of law and philosophy of law up to Kant and Hegel in particular, across the family, civil society, and the state. ...

The tragedy, for it is a tragedy of destiny, is that the two antagonistic terms of this antinomy are not symmetrical. There is a strange hierarchy in this. *The* Law is above the laws. It is thus illegal, transgressive, outside the law, like a lawless law, *nomos anomos*, law above the laws and law outside the law (*anomos*, we remember, that's for instance how Oedipus, the father-son, the son as father, father and brother of his daughters, is characterized). But even while keeping itself above the laws of hospitality, *the* unconditional law of hospitality needs the laws, it *requires* them. This demand is constitutive. It wouldn't be effectively conditional, the law, if it didn't *have to become* effective, concrete, determined, if that were not its being as having-to-be. ...

And vice versa, conditional laws would cease to be laws of hospitality if they were not guided, given inspiration, given aspiration, required, even, by the laws of unconditional hospitality. These two regimes of law, of *the* law and the laws, are thus both contradictory, antinomic, *and* inseparable. They both imply and exclude each other, simultaneously. ...

Because exclusion and inclusion are inseparable in the same moment, whenever you would like to say 'at this very moment', there is antinomy. The law, in the absolute singular, contradicts laws in the plural, but on each occasion it is the law *within* the law, and on each occasion *outside the law* within the law. That's it, that so very singular thing that is called *the* laws of hospitality.[3]

This text is at once extremely subtle and perfectly clear. It supports the welcome of the other as an absolute necessity and juxtaposes this absolute necessity with the relative necessity of the laws of the state.

I would like to make three remarks about Derrida's argument:

- For him (and this is fundamental), the other is *the one who arrives*. This is a serious limitation of the issue. In fact – and we know this from wide-ranging experience – hostility to the other, racism, and xenophobia may well focus on that person's arrival, but they concern just as much, and often even more, the other's presence over the long term, his or her settling in, and the neighbours' coexistence with that person, his or her customs, cultural habits, children ... The notions of welcome, of threshold, of passage are certainly inadequate when it comes to founding an internationalism that would transcend, from inside a country, the baleful preeminence of nationalism.

• The identity of the other, as Derrida thinks it, imposes no limit on this concept. Whether that person is God, a man, a woman, or an animal, otherness alone imposes a law of welcome. But this is an extremely dangerous vision. How are we to accept this absolute imperative when the other is a conquistador, an armed settler looking for something to pillage, a supporter of slavery, or a Zionist preying on Palestinian land? Is it not better to remember here the Madagascan songs set to music by Ravel, where it is said, 'Beware of the white men / You dwellers on the shore'? Do we not see, in the flux of international tourism, the predatory delight of rich westerners going to take the sun in the territories where the most extreme poverty is massive? The ethics of welcome cannot be universalized; it must specify the identity of the one who comes as well as his or her intentions, means, and personal relation to the other, especially in a time like ours, when exotic travel is the favorite entertainment of the western democratic middle classes.

- The relation, which Derrida rightly points to, between the absolute imperative and particular laws remains indeterminate. What are, in fact, most of the laws that seek to control the massive arrival of poor people in rich countries? They are laws having to do with identity, integration, even assimilation, and their goal is to accept only those who are already prepared to obey the norms of the dominant country, to make themselves as invisible as possible outside the work that they are required to provide. As the Madagascan song says, once the 'white men' have been accepted and established in the countries that they want in fact to conquer, they start talking about 'obedience and slavery'. In truth, this is also what they do to new arrivals in their own countries: accept 'our values' and shut up. How can we not see in this case that the absolute law of hospitality is in reality paid for by relative laws that enforce submission and maximum invisibility?

It seems to me in fact that Derrida's intellectual framework and the whole logic of welcome and hospitality actually reduce the new arrival to his or her being as migrant, as nomad, without in any way calling into question the system of dialectical relations between this person's coming, the condition that is his or her own and motivates him or her to come, and the laws that indeed determine this person's acceptance or rejection.

These characteristics, in my view purely negative, of the ethics of migration and welcome also define the orientation of the poetry that accepts the imperative of hospitality as law. The beautiful poems of Laurent Gaudé take their origin from migration itself and from the somehow immediate and sacred contribution of what migration allows us to see. All this continues a sort of sacralization of poverty qua poverty, of its planetary deployment. It is the idea that the procession of the poor, the mistreated, and the humiliated constitutes the gift, for us, of a new sensibility turned towards the universal. Here is an example – the poem 'Look at Them':

> Look at them, these men and women walking in the
>   night,
> They move forward in a single line, along a road that
>   is their blight.
> They are hunched over in fear of the dogs that bite.
> And in their heads,
> Always,
> The incessant din of the countries that have been
>   burned.
> They haven't yet put enough distance between
>   themselves and terror.
> They still hear the knocks on their door.
>
> They still remember being jolted awake at night.
> Look at them.
> A fragile column of men and women
> Moving forward, but always on the lookout,
> They know that danger is everywhere.
> The minutes pass, but the roads are long.
> The hours are days, and the days weeks.
> Birds of prey, in swarms, are on the watch for them.
>   And descend on them.

At the crossroads
They despoil them of their ragged clothing,
And swindle them out of their last tickets.

They say to them: 'More'.
And they give more.
They say to them: 'Still more'.
And they look to the skies, no longer knowing what
    they can give.
Poverty and rags,
Children hanging onto an arm and refusing to talk.
Old parents slowing the pace,
Dragging behind themselves the words of a language
    that they will have to forget.
They move forward. Despite everything.
They persevere
Because they are stubborn?
And then, at last, one day
In a train station,
On a shore,
At the end of one of our roads,
They appear.

Shame on those who see only rags.
Look closely.
They are carrying the light

Of those who are fighting for their lives.
And the gods (if there still are any),
Live within them
So in the night,
From a certain angle, it seems that we are fortunate
    if they are moving toward us.
The column approaches.
It is the place where life is worth living.
There are words that we will learn from hearing
    them speak,
Joys that we will find in their eyes.

Look at them.
They take nothing away from us.
When they spread out their hands,
It is not to beg from us.
It is to offer us
The dream of Europe
That we have forgotten.[4]

You can see that Laurent Gaudé pushes the logic of hospitality to the point of positing that those who come here in this way, through the epic of migration, restore us to ourselves: they give us back the spiritual Europe that material Europe – the Europe of the marketplace – has made us forget. However beautiful and moving the poem may be, what it performs is a sort of digestion, under cover of the word 'migrant', of the wretchedness of those who come here through the supposed 'values' of hospitality and democracy in the countries to which they come.

The poem, here, can and must lead us to the rational analysis of what the word 'migrant' captures only at the most superficial level: forced travel, wretched families, their arrival, the gift that this arrival constitutes for us. The poem, just like the philosopher of hospitality, does not really name the larger context in which this tragedy of wandering is being enacted. Even less does the poem tell us how to combat this tragedy. It rightly advises us to adopt a welcoming attitude, but gives us no help in the struggle to put an end to the need for this unhappy wandering.

The point of departure, which everyone knows without being able to draw the necessary conclusions from it, can be summarized as follows: from now on, in the capitalist universe that organizes the destiny of humanity, the production of anything whatsoever happens on a worldwide, earthwide scale. The manufacture and distribution of a single mobile phone require calculations made in California, financing carried out in US dollars, German technical adjustments, the violent plunder of rare metals in Africa and the South Pacific, painstaking assembly work in vast Chinese factories, and networks of communication established everywhere – all this at the price of ferocious competitive fighting among oligarchic groups of transnational billionaires. Look at Carlos Ghosn: an arrogant billionaire of Lebanese origin, he ran the biggest French factory and is in prison in Japan. A symbol in himself! He, too, has 'migrated'…

We sometimes think of this globalization as a contemporary phenomenon. We speak of 'globalization' as of a wild episode in recent history. Nothing could be further removed from the truth. The capitalist order, the bourgeois oligarchic order, was born from a global vision. It was established from the outset by international commerce, in Venice or in Holland, where colossal fortunes were made, through the mediation of bankers and owners of fleets of ships, on the basis of products from the Far East, Africa, or the Americas. It is this primitive capitalization, this 'accumulation' – this is the technical term – that permitted the massive deployment of wage labour and the enormous profits that the owners of the means of production were able to extract from it.

Here is what, as early as 1848, Marx says about capitalist globalization in the justly famous *Communist Manifesto*:

The need of a constantly expanding market for its products chases the bourgeoisie over the entire surface of the globe. It must nestle everywhere, settle everywhere, establish connections everywhere.

The bourgeoisie has through its exploitation of the world market given a cosmopolitan character to production and consumption in every country. To the great chagrin of Reactionists, it has drawn from under the feet of industry the national ground on which it stood. All old-established national industries have been destroyed or are daily being destroyed. They are dislodged by new industries, whose introduction becomes a life and death question for all civilized nations, by industries that no longer work up indigenous raw material, but raw material drawn from the remotest zones; industries whose products are consumed, not only at home, but in every quarter of the globe. In place of the old wants, satisfied by the production of the country, we find new wants, requiring for their satisfaction the products of distant lands and climes. In place of the old local and national seclusion and self-sufficiency, we have intercourse in every direction, universal inter-dependence of nations. And as in material, so also in intellectual production. The intellectual creations of individual nations become common property. National one-sidedness and narrow-mindedness become more and more impossible, and from the numerous national and local literatures, there arises a world literature.

The bourgeoisie, by the rapid improvement of all instruments of production, by the immensely facilitated means of communication, draws all, even the most barbarian, nations into civilization. The cheap prices of commodities are the heavy artillery with which it batters down all Chinese walls, with which it forces the barbarians' intensely obstinate hatred of foreigners to capitulate. It compels all nations, on pain of extinction, to adopt the bourgeois mode of production; it compels them to introduce what it calls civilization into their midst, i.e., to become bourgeois themselves. In one word, it creates a world after its own image.

The bourgeoisie has subjected the country to the rule of the towns. It has created enormous cities, has greatly increased the urban population as compared with the rural ... Just as it has made the country dependent on the towns, so it has made barbarian and semi-barbarian countries dependent on the civilized ones, nations of peasants on nations of bourgeois, the East on the West.[5]

You will have noted, by the way, that Marx not only describes the conquest of the world by the bourgeois and capitalist system but also includes in this description realities whose omnipresence we can see to this day. For example, the fact that the population is concentrated in enormous cities, the fact that the countryside and the provinces are subjugated to the cities and the capitals, the fact that anything to do with the rural world is in a subordinate position – well, all this can be heard even today, here in France, in the protests of the yellow vests. But what is not heard here, let us mention in passing, is what ought to be the normal conclusion of all this, namely Marx's conclusion: we must work to undo capitalism and to propose an entirely different organization of the global apparatus of production. And I must warn you that the undoing of the mediocre and ignorant Macron by a suspect coalition will not be up to this task.

In the context of globalization, Marx, almost two centuries ago, immediately grasped the need for the wandering of whole masses of people. Here is what he says, still in the *Manifesto*:

> In proportion as the bourgeoisie, i.e., capital, is developed, in the same proportion is the proletariat, the modern working class, developed – a class of labourers, who live only so long as they find work, and who find work only so long as their labour increases capital. These labourers, who must sell themselves piecemeal, are a commodity, like every other article of commerce, and are consequently exposed to all the vicissitudes of competition, to all the fluctuations of the market.
>
> Owing to the extensive use of machinery, and to the division of labour, the work of the proletarians has lost all individual character, and, consequently, all charm for the workman. He becomes an appendage of the machine, and it is only the most simple, most monotonous, and most easily acquired knack, that is required of him. Hence, the cost of production of a workman is restricted, almost entirely, to the means of subsistence that he requires for maintenance, and for the propagation of his race. But the price of a commodity, and therefore also of labour, is equal to its cost of production. In proportion, there-

fore, as the repulsiveness of the work increases, the wage decreases. Nay more, in proportion as the use of machinery and division of labour increases, in the same proportion the burden of toil also increases, whether by prolongation of the working hours, by the increase of the work exacted in a given time or by increased speed of machinery, etc.

Modern industry has converted the little workshop of the patriarchal master into the great factory of the industrial capitalist. Masses of labourers, crowded into the factory, are organized like soldiers. As privates of the industrial army they are placed under the command of a perfect hierarchy of officers and sergeants. Not only are they slaves of the bourgeois class, and of the bourgeois state; they are daily and hourly enslaved by the machine, by the overlooker, and, above all, by the individual bourgeois manufacturer himself. The more openly this despotism proclaims gain to be its end and aim, the more petty, the more hateful and the more embittering it is.[6]

It is important to observe the respective positions of 'proletariat' on the one hand and 'worker' or 'working class' on the other.

A worker is someone who works in the context of the factory, in the context of production organized by capital. I said at the beginning of this book that the majority of those whom we forced to come from Africa to France in the 1950s and 1960s were called 'workers'.

'Proletariat' is a word whose referent is more vast: it designates the mass of those who, merely to survive, must try to become workers, or who are already workers. A proletarian is someone, often a bankrupt or landless farmer, who has only his or her labour power to offer. Such a person is, as Marx says, required to 'sell [him- or herself] piecemeal', and to do so where there is work to be found. 'Worker' refers to work that is localized and determinate. 'Proletarian' is the general condition of someone who has no other possibility of survival than finding work and who, as a result, is 'exposed to all the vicissitudes of competition, to all the fluctuations of the market'.

Today the market, including the labour market, is organized by a planetary oligarchy, according to the strict law of maximum profit. For this reason, there are whole regions where there are no jobs to be had, regions that young people must leave behind, to go wherever jobs are supposed to be and money can be earned and sent to one's family. These young people are, very precisely, proletarians. Insofar as they have not found work, they are necessarily in a state of proletarian wandering; they are nomadic proletarians.

The word 'migrant' makes it look as if the essence of the person we are talking about were to leave, to travel under terrible conditions, and to wind up somewhere. But no! That person's historical essence, itself the result of a capitalist order at the peak of its oppressive inegalitarianism, consists in being forced to become a nomadic proletarian. Let us give this name to the person we are talking about, and let us then understand that our duty is not to welcome this person in the name of an ethics of hospitality. Our duty is to organize ourselves with him or her, with everyone like him or her, if possible at an international level, to prepare the end of the oligarchic world order whose result is his or her being as nomadic proletarian. Which means: our duty is to think and prepare, with this person, the new communist politics.

It is in connection with this figure of the nomadic proletarian that I want to return to poetry. For there is one place in the world, China, where nomadic proletarians remain connected to a communist experience that was interrupted, to be sure, but left many traces. One of these traces is the appearance of a large number of worker poets, poets who were often highly gifted and who invented a new genre: the poetry of workers, which is also often the poetic epic of the nomadic proletariat. These poets tell the story of their migration, from very remote rural provinces in this continent-sized country that is China, provinces that have gradually been deserted, toward the penal colonies of Chinese factories. You probably know that it is these factories that make a prodigious quantity of the consumer products found today all over the world, from saucepans to pants, from telephones to bicycles, from low-cost bedding to highly specialized machine tools. I use the term 'penal colonies' because one finds in them nomadic proletarians who live and work more or less like English workers of a century and a half ago, into whose condition Engels conducted an investigation that was fundamental to the creation of Marxism.

The great contemporary Chinese poet Yang Lian has written an introduction to a collection of poems by the worker Guo Jinniu whose title, significantly, is *Going Home on Paper*.[7] It deals precisely with the question of 'home', as it is asked of nomadic proletarians. Wandering dissolves the stability of 'home'. And our only recourse is to build a sort of universal 'home', to which the poem is the true witness.

In his introduction, Yang Lian briefly describes the world of the gigantic workers' migration in contemporary China:

> a world of mutes: villages abandoned by innumerable young people who turned their backs on their homes, bewildering cities, barren as deserts, the degrading work environment of the labourers in the lowest strata of society, and also their state of mind, so much more desolate and miserable than the world around them.[8]

Under these circumstances, 'What is home?' and 'Where is my house?' become essential questions. And Guo Jinniu's answer, Yang Lian tells us, is this:

> Deep feelings and truth expressed, these are our home. They are rooted in our hearts by every line of poetry. Seen this way, which of us is not on the way back home? Going home on paper – the inexhaustible return home, a return to the poetical consanguinity which has linked true life to true language since time immemorial.[9]

Here is the very beginning of a poem by Guo Jinniu, magnificently titled 'A Massively Singular Number' and thus naming, with great precision, the possible infinite singularity of what holds an essential truth in reserve:

> A person crossed a province, another province, and
>   another province
> A person took a train, a coach, and then a black
>   bus
> Next stop
>
> Our Motherland, it organized me a Temporary
>   Residence Permit.
> Our Motherland, it accepted the Temporary
>   Residence Fee I handed over.

And then, a little later in the poem:

> 'Little white cabbage, tears streaming down'.
> Someone in the south broke into a rented room
> Oh god. It's a raid to check Temporary Residence
>   Permits.[10]

You see how Guo Jinniu poeticizes, with a sort of insistent sobriety, the combination of two fundamental questions that are linked, throughout the world, to the movements of nomadic proletarians: the question of travel and the question of identification papers.

For the nomadic proletarian, there is always and everywhere the all-consuming question of papers, of what Jacques Rancière rightly calls the 'red tape of the poor': visas on passports, various certificates, summonses to appear at the local prefecture, temporary residence permits, deportation decrees, documents to provide proofs of age, sex, origin, level of education, knowledge of the language – and so forth.

Once again, there is nothing new here: since the nineteenth century France has had a 'worker's booklet', which gives the nomadic proletarian the right, subject to surveillance and cancellation, to live where there is work, especially in Paris, and thus a chance to become a worker. All it takes is one minor slip-up for the booklet to be revoked and for the worker to find him- or herself back in the position of a nomadic proletarian ordered to return home.

Having become the largest workers' country in the world, China immediately created its own worker's booklet, the Temporary

Residence Permit, along with a whole police apparatus to oversee it, as evoked in the final lines: 'It's a raid to check Temporary Residence Permits'.

Here is one more example of the nomadic proletarian's search for poetic salvation – this time a poem by Xin You, who raises the question of his very being as nomadic proletarian and asks 'Who exactly are we, we workers?' given that nomadism is inevitable. Here is this remarkable poem:

We who have no fixed dwellings
We who make our homes wherever we happen to
    be,
We who abandoned our native villages
We who drift from place to place
We who live a life of wandering

We who appeared suddenly on the yellow earth
We who in order to live
Betrayed the yellow earth
We who struggle in cities
Our sweat a gift and our youth
Flowing drop by drop
Often excluded as foreigners

We who scatter toward the east and toward the west
We who live in cities
But whom they still call 'peasants'
We who coming back home
Find nothing that is familiar to us anymore
We who can do two different things at once
Stuck as we are in between the two
We who are abandoned
And who then in the middle of the spring in the
    first lunar month
Go back as quickly as possible one by one toward
    the south

And who are we, exactly?
Who, exactly, are we?

We, workers,
We who work throughout the seasons
We who are like birds
Migrators who have lost everything,

We are the 'Lame Ducks'.[11]

We could take this magnificent poem as a conclusion. We can conceive of our role as one of
responding to this question: 'Who are we, we

workers in China and in all other places, under the yoke of our being as nomadic proletarians?' And let us answer: 'You are and will be, in your land of origin as in your adopted land, those who embody universality, those who will help us give birth to the unified world of the new communism. May your terrible experience give birth to something that will change you from lame ducks to Annunciation storks!'

But I would like to end on an even more lyrical note.

For this is indeed what we find at the end of Chamoiseau's *Migrant Brothers*, even if 'migrant' is not the appropriate word, even if the poeticizing ethics of welcome and hospitality is too present. One actually finds at the end of the book a 'poets' declaration', which is like the charter that, in the voice of poetry, nomadic proletarians summon us to sign. Its universalist impulse is convincing and can resonate within us for a long time – all the more so as the declaration concludes with an emphasis on the unconditional, absolute necessity of no longer tolerating drownings and mass arrests, restrictions of all kinds, the 'red tape of the poor', and the exclusion of this or that person for wretched and obscene reasons that have to do with his or her origin or status. Here are the five final articles of this solemn declaration of poets:

9 The poets declare that a National or Supranational Constitution that would not anticipate welcoming procedures for those who visit, come, and call out would contravene the Safety of all.

10 The poets declare that no refugee, seeker of asylum, migrant by necessity, voluntary exile, no poetically displaced person can appear in any place in this world without having not one face but all faces, not one heart but all hearts, not one soul but all souls. That they are therefore a product of the Deep History of all our histories, that they therefore incarnate the history of our histories, and consequently become an absolute symbol of human dignity.

11 The poets declare that never again will anyone on this planet have to set foot on a foreign land – every land will be native to all – nor will anyone remain in the margins of citizenship – every citizenship conferring on all its graces – and that citizenship, caring for the world's

diversity, cannot decide what cultural luggage and tools it might wish to choose.

12 The poets declare that, whatever the circumstances, a child cannot be born outside of childhood; that childhood is the salt of the earth, the soil of our soil, the blood of all bloods, that childhood is thus everywhere at home, like the breathing of the wind, the salubrity of the storm, the fertility of lightning, always the priority, plenary from the start, and automatically a citizen.

13 The poets declare that the entire Mediterranean is henceforth a place of homage to those who died there, that its shores provide the foundations for a celebratory arch, open to the winds and open to the faintest of lights, spelling out for all the letters of the word WELCOME, in every language, in every melody, and this word plainly constitutes the ethics of the living world.[12]

This final appeal touches me all the more today because, I must confess to you, one thing in particular has kept me at a distance from the so-called movement of the yellow vests: the massive presence, the constant reappearance, of the dreary French flag, the sight of which never fails to oppress me, and of a Marseillaise that too many fascist-leaning nationalisms have struck up for us to remember its revolutionary origins any more. We often heard, in recent discussions of the 'movement', the remark apropos of inadequate pensions, cancelled public services, reduced buying power: 'Who would have thought that things like these could ever happen in France?' This remark can never express anything but the bitterness of someone who thought that he or she was superior, and therefore protected from the planetary gangsterism of capital, whose ravages across entire continents were, and are, violent in different ways from what has been the case in our little country, even though it is reaching the end of its historic run. In the mental maintenance of this tattered sense of superiority, I hear all too well that, rather than 'beware of white men' – which we should be hearing, and by which I mean 'beware of the system they invented and spread everywhere by force' – what we are hearing is 'beware of blacks, Arabs, Asians, and 'migrants' of all kinds'.

Yes, after all I agree – I agree wholeheartedly, and I ask you to agree actively – to there being a world in which 'never again will anyone on this planet have to set foot on a foreign land', for 'every land will be native to all'. As a result, nobody will ask a nomadic proletarian to wave a national flag of any colour or stripe, as a requirement for his or her presence, for his or her lively conviction, and for his or her decisive influence on moving towards what I myself call the new communism but am happy to see described by the poet as the 'ethics of the living world'.

Notes

1 Recording of an oral statement transcribed by Mediapart (in French). Unless otherwise specified, all the quotations in this book are translated by Joseph Litvak from the original French edition.

2 Patrick Chamoiseau, *Migrant Brothers: A Poet's Declaration of Human Dignity*, trans. Matthew Amos and Frederik Rönnbäck (New Haven, CT: Yale University Press, 2018), 3–4.

3 Jacques Derrida, 'Step of Hospitality/No Hospitality'. In Anne Dufourmantelle and Jacques Derrida, *Of Hospitality: Anne Dufourmantelle Invites Jacques Derrida to Respond*, trans. Rachel Bowlby (Stanford, CA: Stanford University Press, 2000), 77–81.

4 Laurent Gaudé, 'Regardez-les'. The poem was published in the weekly *Le 1* (73), 9 September 2015, which is available online at https://le1hebdo.fr/

journal/numero/73. In order to read the poem on this site, one must register and sign in, although no payment is required. A PDF of the poem in French is more readily accessible at http://projetasylum.blogspot.com/2017/04/regardez-les-de-laurent-gaude-avec.html.

5 Karl Marx and Friedrich Engels, *Manifesto of the Communist Party*, trans. Samuel Moore in cooperation with Friedrich Engels (Moscow: Progress Publishers, 1969), 16–17. https://www.marxists.org/archive/marx/works/download/pdf/Manifesto.pdf.

6 Marx and Engels, *Manifesto*, 18.

7 [Translator's note: This collection is part of an anthology gathered, translated, and edited by Yang Lian under the title *A Massively Single Number*, which is the title of Guo Jinniu's opening poem.]

8 Yang Lian, ed., *A Massively Single Number*, trans. Brian Holton (Bristol: Shearsman Books, 2015), 113.

9 Lian, *A Massively Single Number*, 113–14.

10 Guo Jinniu, 'A Massively Single Number', from his collection *Going Home on Paper*, edited by Yang Lian in his anthology (Lian, *A Massively Single Number*), 150–1. Original poem copyright © Guo Jinniu, 2015; translation copyright © Brian Holton, 2015. Reproduced here by kind permission of Shearsman Books.

11 [Translator's note: Unpublished text, translated here from the French version in Badiou's text, whose provenance has not been established.]

12 Chamoiseau, *Migrant Brothers*, 117–18.